Golf for Beginners:
The Offical Survival Guide

Getting started in golf
without having a stroke

by

Scott J. Lotts
and
Vicki Barnes-Rothmeier

Mulligan's Press, Ltd.
Ann Arbor, Michigan
USA

Design and layout by Vicki Rothmeier
Graphics by: Vicki Rothmeier, Corel Draw, 3G Graphics,
            Image Club, One Mile Up, Inc.,
            Totem Graphics, TNT Designs

Library of Congress Cataloging-in-Publication Data
Barnes-Rothmeier, Vicki
Lotts, Scott
Golf for Beginners: The Official Survival Guide
    Vicki Barnes-Rothmeier
    Scott Lotts

ISBN 0-09645700-0-9
Printed in USA, Third edition, 1999
10   9   8   7   6   5   4

Thanks to my husband Ross for all his support and love.

Vicki

Mom and Turner, thanks for being there for me. Your smiles and love are contagious.

Scott

Acknowledgements

Thanks to: Ross Rothmeier, Gregg Rasmussen,
and James Lotts, Jr. for the great ideas.
Thanks also to John Michalik for the
editing help.

Thanks also to our families and friends for
their continuing support.

Mulligan's Press books are available at special dis-
counts for bulk purchases, sales promotions, fund-
raising, or educational use. For details contact:
Business Manager,
Mulligan's Press, Ltd.
5680 Thomas Road
Ann Arbor, MI 48108

Table of Contents

Introduction

Let the games begin

The game of golf 4
  Object of the game 5
  Rules 5
  Before you go to the course tips 6
  Etiquette 7
  On the course 11
  The scorecard 13
  Good lies and bad lies 14
  The tee box 15
  The fairway 16
  The rough 17
  Hazards 17
  The green 19
  Putting 20
  Etiquette on the green 21

Scoring and games

Scoring golf games 26
  What's par? 26
  Aces, eagles, birdies, par, and bogies 27
Handicap 28
  Individual handicap 28
  Official handicap 29
  Figuring your unofficial handicap 29
  Who won? 29
  Hole handicap 30
Golf games 31
  Stroke play 31
  Skins 31
  Match play 31
  Scramble 32
  Best ball 32
  Nassau 33

Starting to swing

Driving range 36
Before you start swinging 37
  Addressing the ball 37
  Posture 37
  Stance 38
  Grip 39
Taking a swing 40
  Backswing and takeaway 41
  Downswing and impact 42
  Follow through 43
  Swing checklist 44
Short Game 46
  What kind of chip shot do I use? 46
    A. The lob shot 47
    B. The chip shot 47
    C. The chip and run 47
What about golf lessons? 48
  Finding a good instructor 48
  Getting the most from your lessons 49

What club do I use?

Choosing the right club for the shot 52
  Approximate club distance 53
Specialty clubs 54
  Specialty irons 54
  Specialty woods 55

Golf equipment and buying tips

Selecting equipment 58
  Golf bags 58
  Golf gloves 59
  Clothing 59
  Golf balls 60
  Shoes 62

Table of Contents

Golf equipment and buying tips, continued

Golf clubs **63**

    Club anatomy 65

        Grip 65

        Golf club shaft 66

        Club head 68

    Before buying clubs 69

A field trip to the pro shop **70**

    Buying irons and woods 71

Golf rules

Common rules **74**

    Water hazards 76

    Regular water hazards 77

    Lateral water hazards 77

    Playing by the rules 79

Words of wisdom and Golf lingo

    Words of wisdom 82

    Golf bag goodies 86

    Golf lingo 87

Table of Contents

Introduction
Golf for Beginners: The Official Survival Guide
-- or -- Getting started playing golf without having a stroke.

Golf is one of those progressive pleasures. As you progress from one stage to another, you find more pleasures. In plain English, the more you play golf, the more you'll enjoy it.

The story on the back cover is true. We wrote this book to help the beginning golfer feel comfortable playing the game. We cover what happens on the golf course, customs of etiquette, scoring and games, how to buy equipment, and give you the lingo you'll need to know. There are also pointers and tips all along the way. And, we found that many of our readers who wouldn't consider themselves beginning golfers learned lots of useful information too. We kept hearing, "Hey, I didn't know that".

While the commercials try to convince you that golf is about power drives and crushing your opponent, that really isn't the case at all. Golf is more about finesse, accuracy, sportsman-ship, and improving your own game. After all, a 3-foot putt counts the same as a 300-yard drive. This makes golf a great game for people of all ages and sizes.

And everyone on the planet plays by the same rules. Wherever you go, you can meet new people and have fun. Maybe this is why the sport has grown into a worldwide pastime.

Golf was at one time considered a rich man's sport. Now, everyone enjoys the game.

We're sure you will too.

This section explains who's to credit (or blame) for the game of golf.

This section also covers the object of the game, some tips on etiquette, and what to do on the golf course.

1

Let the games begin

The game of golf

Golf is an ancient game whose history is believed to have started with the Romans.

But it's the Scots who are credited with (or blamed for) making the object of the game to hit a small ball into a hole. Golf became so popular with the Scots that in the mid 1400s, King James worried that his archers were playing too much golf and neglecting their military practice. He banned golf in Scotland for a time and instructed his troops to practice their military skills instead. Some historians question about how well the ban worked. There is some speculation about the part that the golf craze played in the defeat of the Scots by the British.

Some golf terms have their roots in the early history of the game. Many early golf courses were sheep pastures that were not fit for grazing cattle. These pastures were between the better pastures and the sea, and were called the links. You'll hear the term golf links today as a reference to a golf course. Or, players would play golf on the village green -- that's where the term green or playing through the green comes from. Modern terminology is sometimes just as obscure. Check out the Golf lingo section in the back of the book for more information.

Object of the game

The object of golf is to use a club to hit the ball
into a hole using as few strokes as possible.
Winston Churchill is said to have described golf as
a game where the object is "to hit a very small ball
into an even smaller hole with weapons singularly
ill-designed for the purpose". Some days we agree.

Rules

The rules of golf have changed little over the years.
Today's rules of golf are gov-
erned jointly by two groups:
The Royal and Ancient Golf
Club of St. Andrews in
Scotland (R&A), and the
United States Golf Asso-
ciation (USGA). Every 4
years, the R&A and the
USGA meet to review the
rules, proposals for amendments and changes, and
approve new equipment. All national golf organiza-
tions, whether professional or amateur, follow the
official rules.

We explain some of the most common USGA rules
in Section 6. For a more comprehensive explanation of rules and special situations (yes, there's
even a rule for what to do if your ball is moved by
an earthquake or eaten by an animal), read an
Official USGA Rules of Golf book.

Tips to know before going to the course

Here are a few suggestions that will help you get started playing golf.

Tip: You might want to practice on the driving range before you hit the golf course. See the Starting to swing section for information on the driving range and some tips on swinging the club.

Tip: Ask someone who has played on a golf course to go with you the first time you play. They can help you get around on the course your first time out.

Tip: Call the course to make sure that it's a good course for beginners. You might want to find what's called an Executive Golf Course to start out on. The distance of each hole on an Executive Course is usually shorter than on regular golf courses -- which may be more fun at first.

Tip: Call the course at least a few days in advance to reserve a time to play your round. This starting time is called the **tee time**. You may need to give your credit card number to reserve a tee time. And, check to see if you'll be charged if you miss your tee time and don't cancel ahead. This is also a good time to ask about the fees, method of payment, and rain checks.

Tip: If you don't own clubs, you may be able to rent a set at the golf course or at a golf shop.

Etiquette

Since golf can be not only a sport, but a social situation, knowing the customs of etiquette is as important as knowing the rules of the game. (Some people feel that walking in someone's line when they are putting a hanging offense. We explain what this means later.) When you go to a new course, ask if there are any special course rules. Many localities have their own accent on etiquette. Here are a few of the more common customs.

Wear the right clothes - Color coordination doesn't seem to be very important in golf clothes, judging from some of the golf outfits we've seen. However, folks don't expect to see any body parts they're not used to seeing in public. Generally, you shouldn't wear tank tops or short-shorts -- concentration being an important part of the game and all. In fact, some courses are pretty picky about what you can wear. If you're playing at a private club you might want to ask if there is a dress code.

Make sure you're on time for the tee - You'll want to be ready to play at least 15 minutes before your tee time. The course folks may skip you if you're late, and the course management may expect you to pay for a missed tee time.

Speed of play - 2 1/4 hours is considered average for 9 holes, but be prepared to pick up the pace on the weekends when the courses are busy. You can help the game go faster by being ready to hit the ball when it's your turn.

Renting a cart - Renting a cart is another way to speed up the game. Courses usually have pull carts that you put your golf bag on and pull around. If you rent a riding cart, try to be a careful driver. It's considered bad form to run over other golfers, no matter how badly they beat you. And, you can be prepared to shell out big cash if you drive the golf cart across the green or in the sand trap. The course management will ask you to pay for damages. Generally you'll be safe if you stay on the path. Ask the folks in the course pro shop where you're allowed to drive the cart.

Mulligan's Acres

Talking on the course - They say that a lot of business gets done on the golf course. But, we don't know many folks who enjoy conversation while they're trying to concentrate on hitting the ball.

What would your mother say if she heard you using foul language or saw you throwing your clubs? Chances are someone will hear what you say and see what you do -- be sure to mind your manners.

Give people their space - No, this isn't an idea that's leftover from the seventies. For safety and for courtesy, you don't want to stand directly behind or in front of anyone who is swinging at the ball.

Yelling fore - There is one time where you should yell on the golf course. If you hit a golf ball in the direction of other people, yell FORE to warn them to duck or get out of the way.

Replace divots - When you watch golf on TV, you'll see sod flying everywhere. This sod in the air is called a divot, because as part of your swing, you literally take a divot of grass out of the course when you hit the ball. You're generally supposed to put the divot back.

Northern courses usually ask you to put the divot back where it came from and step on it to help the roots get started again.

Some southern courses give you a little bag of sand and grass seed to put in the hole. To find out what to do, look on the score card, ask the starter (the person who directs you to the first tee), or ask at clubhouse before you head out.

Rake the bunkers (sand traps) - If the gods of golf send you to the bunker, be sure to rake it smooth after you get out. Others who anger the bunker gods will appreciate your thoughtfulness.

Let others play through if you play slowly -
If there is no one on the hole in front of you, and the folks behind you seem to be waiting for your group to finish a hole frequently, ask if they'd like to play through. Letting someone play through is like letting someone go ahead of you in the line at the grocery.

Let people play through:

O if you have a foursome and the group behind you has fewer members,

O if the group behind is using golf carts and you're not, or

O if they seem to spend a lot of time waiting for you because they play faster than you.

To let another group play through, wait until you're at the next tee and ask if they'd like to tee off before your group does. It's considered to be very courteous to let others play through if you play slowly.

On the course

When you get to the golf course, go to the clubhouse first to check in and pay your greens fees. The clubhouse folks will give you a scorecard and tell you where to find the first hole. Remember to get a pencil.

There is usually a map of the course on the score card that looks something like this one. The map shows you how to find your way around and where the hazards are.

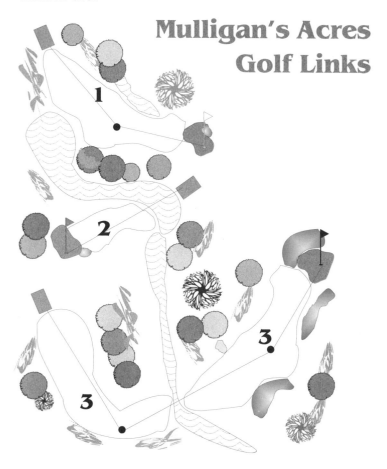

Mulligan's Acres Golf Links

1

2

3

3

The course map may be hard to figure out at first. We've taken the third hole from Mulligan's Acres and labeled the different parts. Each part is explained in more detail later in the chapter.

3rd Hole

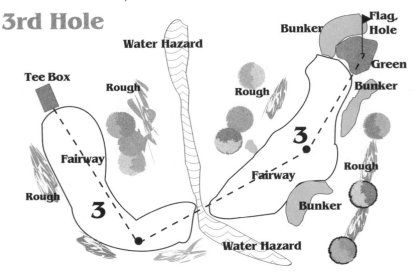

A short introduction:

The **tee box** is where you start each hole.

Because the grass is very smooth on the **fairway**, you want to hit the ball there as much as possible.

There are 2 kinds of **water hazards**; regular and lateral. Water hazards can cause you penalty strokes.

A **bunker** is a hole filled with sand. It's also called a **sandtrap** or folks who have spent a lot of time in them call them **the beach**. Try to stay out if you can.

The **green** is where you putt the ball into the hole.

The **flag** or **pin** marks where the hole is on the green.

The **rough** is all the heavy or tall grass around the fairways.

The **dashed lines** with the big number 3s show the best way to play the hole. The expected score (**par**) for this hole is 5; 3 strokes to get on the green, and 2 to putt.

The scorecard

Write the number of strokes that you take per hole on the scorecard. This example scorecard is filled out for the first few holes. The players' names and scores are in green.

Hole	1	2	3	4	5	6	7	8	9	Out
Blue Tees	400	195	377	403	423	394	531	392	191	3306
White Tees	395	185	373	392	421	387	530	389	185	3257
Handicap	6	8	5	3	2	4	1	9	7	
Par	4	3	4	4	4	4	5	4	3	35
Scott	4	2	5							
Vicki	4	3	4							
Ross	4	6	4							
Turner	3	4	4							
+ or -										
Red Tees	335	161	338	319	407	367	488	359	168	2942
Par	4	3	4	4	5	4	5	4	3	36

A. The hole number.

B. The distance from the tee to the hole.

C. The hole handicap. Each hole is ranked according to difficulty, with 1 being the hardest.

D. The hole par is the number of strokes it should take a proficient player to finish the hole.

E. The players' names and scores.

F. The out column holds totals for the first 9 holes of play.

+ or - Match play, scramble, or best ball scores.

Good lies and bad lies

One thing that makes golf interesting is that you must play the golf ball where it lands (called the lie). If the ball lands somewhere inconvenient, it is called a bad lie.

You can make a bad lie work for you by blaming bad shots on the terrible lie you had to shoot from. You can also blame the sun, wind, rain, ball, your boss and/or spouse.

Sometimes during tournaments when the course is in bad shape, the officials may allow players to **pick, clean,** and **place** their golf ball. These terms mean that players may mark the ball, pick it up and clean it, and place it as close to the original lie as possible.

Also, although it's not sanctioned, your group may decide to allow players to move the ball a bit to get a good lie for the next shot. This is often called **playing winter rules.**

When the courses are in better shape, folks generally play the game as it is intended; playing each ball where it lies. If you can't play a ball where it lies, you may be forced to take a penalty stroke. Some of the most common rules and penalties are explained in the Golf rules section.

The tee box

The tee box is where you begin each hole. This is the only place on the course where you're allowed to use a tee. The tee holds the ball off the ground so it's easier to hit. The original tee was a little mound of sand that the golfer put on the ground to hold the ball up. Today's tees serve the same purpose and are made of wood, plastic, or biodegradable materials.

You must start your shot from inside the tee box. This graphic shows the markers you'll find inside the tee box. There won't be an outline around the tee box but generally, the grass is longer outside the tee box than inside it.

Tee marker color	Used by
Red	Ladies
Yellow	Seniors
White	Intermediate
Blue	Advanced
Gold	Pro

The graphic shows the tee markers all within one box. Out on the course, they will be at different distances from the green. Be sure to tee up somewhere between and behind one of the sets of markers -- but not farther back than 2 club lengths from the front of that set.

The fairway

As you look out over the golf course, you'll see areas of short grass that sort of lead the way to the green. This area is called the fairway. Because the fairway is carefully maintained, you'll want to keep your ball on it to avoid hazards and to stay out of the rough -- giving you the best chance of getting a good lie. The fairway is not always the shortest distance from the tee box to the green, but staying on it can keep you out of trouble and help keep your scores lower.

Yardage markers - The yardage markers on the fairway tell you how far you are from the hole as you approach the green. Ask the starter or the people in the pro shop where to find the yardage markers.

This little table gives you an idea of which club to use. There's a more complete table in Section 4.

Approximate shot distance in yards

Club	Men	Ladies
Irons		
3	195	155
5	165	125
7	135	95
9	105	65
Pitching wedge	90	50
Woods		
1 (driver)	235	195
3	195	175

The rough

Longer grass and rough terrain make hitting

shots out of the rough more difficult. The longer grass slows the momentum of the club at impact, so shots out of heavy rough usually don't go as far as shots hit from the fairway.

Hazards

The deviant folks who design hazards make them out of water, sand, and other undesirable terrain. Sometimes you'll see markers around the outside of the hazard. If your ball lands on the border or inside these markers, it is considered to be in the hazard. There are lots of rules about what you can do inside a hazard -- see the Rules of golf section for more information.

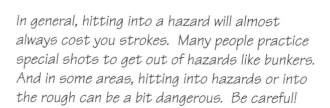

In general, hitting into a hazard will almost always cost you strokes. Many people practice special shots to get out of hazards like bunkers. And in some areas, hitting into hazards or into the rough can be a bit dangerous. Be careful!

Short game

As you get closer to the green, there are times when you need to adjust your swing and hit short shots. This is called the short game. The two places you'll use the short game strokes most are when you are hitting the ball onto the green from a short distance away (**chipping**) and when you are putting.

Chipping

Use a chip shot when the ball is fairly close to the green (within 40 yards). The club and stroke you use are determined by the path you want the ball to take.

A good chip shot puts the ball in the cup or at least as close to the cup as possible. This graphic shows one of the most common chip shots. The kind of chip shot you use is mostly determined by the terrain and the speed of the green.

We spend more time explaining chipping and the different chip shots in Section 3, Swinging the club. The most important thing to remember about the short game is that practicing chipping and putting will pay off in lower scores. There are some putting tips following the explanation of the green.

The green

Greens can be different shapes and sizes. You'll hear the terms "fast green", or "slow green" to describe how fast the ball rolls across the green. Briefly, the shorter the grass, the faster the ball will travel. Other things that affect the speed are water on the green, its terrain, and even the direction the grass grows (called the **grass grain**). As you play golf more often, you'll learn how to **read the greens**.

The flag is also called the pin. Because the people who run the golf courses move the cup to a different spot on the green every few days, some golf courses give you a little map (**pin sheet**) that locates the hole the green. Or, some golf courses put a ball or a little flag on the pin to help you gauge where the cup is on the green. If the pin location marker is toward the:

O top of the pin, the hole is at the back of the green.

O middle of the pin, the hole is near the center of the green.

O bottom of the pin, the hole is at the front of the green.

Many golf matches are won and lost on the green. And, there are probably more rules about the green than anywhere else on the course. The next few pages explain about putting and etiquette on the green.

Putting

You can use any club to hit the ball onto the green. But once on the green, you'll use the putter to hit the ball into the hole. We've spoken about golf being a game of finesse. Nowhere is this more true than when you are putting. Because a three-foot put counts the same as a three-hundred yard drive -- putting is the great equalizer. There's a wonderful saying, "You drive for show, but you putt for dough". Believe it, because it's true.

The grass on the green is very short, and looks very smooth. But don't be fooled. Because the grass is so short, your ball will follow every curve in the terrain. When lining up (aiming) a putt, pay attention to the slope of the green. Decide how hard you need to hit the ball, and try to pick the best path (line) for your putt.

Putting tips

Tip: Stand over the ball so you look directly down on it.

Tip: Use a smooth stroke where the backswing is as long as the follow through.

Tip: Try to hit the ball just hard enough so it's travelling slowly by the time it drops into the hole. This is called dying into the hole. If the ball is dying into the hole, gravity might pull it into the cup even if the putt is a bit off. If the ball is travelling quickly, momentum will carry it past the hole.

Etiquette on the green

There are so many etiquette customs associated with the green, we feel that it deserves its own section.

Try to remember to keep your golf bag off the green. Because a golf bag is sometimes pretty heavy, it can leave a not-so-favorable impression on the green and throw someone's putt off line. This can happen whether you carry the bag across the green, or lay the bag on it.

If you lay your golf bag and any clubs you're not using off the green in a path on the way to the next tee, you'll save yourself steps, speed up the game, and keep from forgetting clubs.

If your ball makes an indentation when it lands on the green, you'll need to fix the ball mark. Use a divot tool or a tee to lift the indentation and then tap the area smooth with you putter.

Who putts first? As with any other part of the golf course, the person farthest from the hole putts first. This is called having the honor. The person can either complete the putt (putt out) or let the next person who is farthest from the hole putt.

Be careful not to walk in anyone else's line. The line is the path between where the golf ball is sitting and the hole. If you walk in someone's line, you may indent the green and cause their putt to swerve unexpectedly -- and miss the cup. Guaranteeing dirty looks.

Golf for Beginners:

When do I move the flag? Usually, the last person to putt (whose golf ball is closest to the hole) tends the flag. When you tend the flag, the first thing you do is ask the person who is putting if they can see the hole. If they can see the hole, go ahead and take the flag out of the cup (called **pulling the pin**).

If the person can't see the hole, wait until their putt is about halfway to the cup and then pull the pin. It's a 2-stroke penalty if their golf ball hits the flag when they are putting on the green.

If you lay the flag down on the green, be sure it's out of everyone's way. The 2-stroke penalty for hitting the flag counts whether the pin is in the cup or lying down on the green.

The first person to putt out usually takes over the flag tending duties and is responsible for seeing that the flag is replaced when everyone finishes the hole.

What if my ball is in someone's line? While people don't always practice this point, it's considered most polite to mark your ball as soon as everyone in your group reaches the green. Place a coin or a ball marker directly behind the ball. The smaller and flatter the marker the better. Folks can't putt around a hockey puck.

When it's your turn to play, put the golf ball back in front of the marker, pick the marker up, and then putt.

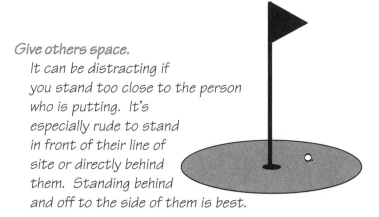

Give others space.
It can be distracting if
you stand too close to the person
who is putting. It's
especially rude to stand
in front of their line of
site or directly behind
them. Standing behind
and off to the side of them is best.

Mum's the word. Well, actually, it's more polite to
be quiet and not move around when someone is
putting.

After everyone in your group has finished putting,
move quickly off the green and mark your score
cards on the way to or on the next tee. This
speeds up the game, and the players behind
you will really appreciate it.

Another great feature of golf is that there are many different games you can play.

This section explains scoring and how to play some of the games.

2

Scoring and games

Scoring golf games

Most games are played on a golf course using standard golf equipment; the differences in the games come in the scoring. The two scoring terms you hear most often are *par* and *handicap*.

What's par?

When a course is designed, the resident expert figures out how many strokes it should take a proficient player to complete the hole. This is called par. Actually, the concept of par is the backbone of the game. When you play golf, you're really playing against par.

Par	Men average distance	Ladies average distance
3	180 yards	120 yards
4	390 yards	330 yards
5	510 yards	450 yards

Par for most 18-hole golf courses is between 70 and 72. You can tell others your score in golf lingo in terms of how many strokes you took to play the course -- *I shot an 85.* Or you can tell them how many strokes above or below par you took -- *I shot 13 over.*

Aces, eagles, birdies, par and bogies

Most golf scoring is based on how close your score is to par. This table shows the different terms for scores and their relationship to par.

 Ace - Hole in One

 Double Eagle - 3 under par

 Eagle - 2 under par

 Birdie - 1 under par

 Even par

 **Bogey** - 1 over par

 Double Bogey - 2 over par

 Triple Bogey - 3 over par

 Quadruple Bogey - 4 over par

Handicap

The handicapping system is pretty complicated.
In fact, the USGA puts out a 100 page book that
explains all the details. Here, we'll just try to give
you a basic understanding.

There are 2 types of handicaps: your individual
handicap and the hole handicap.

Your **individual handicap** gauges how close your
average score is to par or to the course rating.
When people ask you what your handicap is,
they're referring to this number.

The **hole handicap** is a clue to the difficulty of a
particular hole on the golf course. Each hole and
its handicap is listed on the scorecard. The hole
is rated in difficulty -- 1 through 9 for 9-hole golf
courses, or 1 through 18 for an 18-hole course.
The lower the number, the more difficult the hole
is considered to be.

Individual handicap

The individual handicap is used to even the playing
field in scoring so people of
all skill levels can play together. Basically, your handicap is the difference between your
average score and the course
rating or course par.
If a golf course is not rated,
you can figure your handicap
using the course par.

Official handicap

Your official handicap is calculated by a service that figures handicaps for the USGA. When you start playing in tournaments, you'll need to have an official USGA handicap. See your course pro for more information.

Figuring your unofficial handicap

To figure your unofficial handicap, subtract the number of strokes listed on the scorecard as the course rating (if the course is not rated, use the course par) from the number of strokes you took to complete the course. The resulting number is your handicap.

$$
\begin{array}{r}
\text{Your score} \\
-\ \underline{\text{Course rating (or par)}} \\
=\ \text{Unofficial handicap}
\end{array}
$$

After a few games, add up the handicap numbers and divide that number by the number of games you've played. This more accurate (but still unofficial) number is your new handicap. Your goal is to beat your handicap as often as you can. It's a good gauge of how your game is improving.

Who won?

At the end of the round, you add up all your strokes. Then subtract your handicap to produce your score. The person with the lowest net score wins.

$$
\begin{array}{r}
\text{Your score} \\
-\ \underline{\text{Your handicap}} \\
=\ \text{Net score}
\end{array}
$$

Hole handicap

The hole handicap tells the difficulty of a hole compared with the other holes on the course. Holes are rated with the hardest hole considered handicap #1. The handicap number is for your information and doesn't have anything to do with your score unless you're playing a match play handicap tournament.

Course rating - The course rating is a number that takes into account which tees the golfer uses (men's, ladies, senior or pro), and the difficulty of the course. The higher the course rating, the harder the course is. When you call for a tee time, you might want to ask about the course rating. A course rating of 70.0 or below is usually considered a good course for beginners.

Course par - Find the course par by adding up the par numbers on the scorecard for each hole.

The handicap system is basically an honor system. Accurately reporting your handicap and playing an honest game upholds the foundation and tradition of the game.

Golf games

Stroke play, Skins, Match play, Scramble, Nassau, and Best ball are some of the most popular golf games. The next couple of pages explain how to play and score these games. Like in cards, there may be rules for these games that are different from course to course (like house rules). It's always a good idea to agree on the rules before you start the round.

Stroke play

Count each stroke taken during the round of 9 or 18 holes. The lowest net score wins. Stroke play is the most popular way to play golf.

Skins

Skins games are usually played in a foursome for a prize agreed upon by the players. (Legend says that the name of the game came from the skins that were used for prizes -- animal pelts that the winner could sell.) The lowest score for each hole wins a skin. If there is a tie, no one wins the skin. Or, you can carry the skin over to the next hole so that the winner of that hole wins twice as much.

Match Play

Count each stroke taken for each hole. The player who takes the fewest number of strokes wins that hole. The player who wins the most holes wins the match. There are special rules for handicapping in match play. Ask the course pro or see a handicapping book for more information.

Scramble

Scramble is a game of 2 to 4 players per team. After each person tees off, the team decides which shot was best. Everyone hits their next shot from that spot. At the end of the round, the team with the lowest scramble score wins.

Scramble is one of the most popular team games in golf. It's a good game to play at outings where players of different skill levels are participating.

Best ball

This game is also played in teams of 2 to 4 players. Everyone plays their own ball and tallies up their individual score for the hole. At the end of each hole, the team score-keeper records the best individual score -- which then becomes the team score.

At the end of the round, the lowest team score wins.

Nassau

You only play 1 round of golf, but you keep track of your scores for the front 9, for the back 9, and your total. Each 9-hole score counts as a separate game. It's possible to win the competition for the front 9, lose the competition for the back 9, but still win for total score.

That's what makes playing Nassau so much fun. It ain't over till it's over.

Figuring in your handicap

In the games where handicap is counted, all players add up their strokes at the end of the round and then subtract their handicap to produce their net score. The player with the lowest net score wins.

Of course, it's a good idea that everyone agrees on the scoring method before starting to play.

This section tells you about
going to the driving
range and practicing
all parts of your swing.

3

Starting to swing

Driving range

The range is a great place to learn how to hit the golf ball. We recommend that you practice at the driving range at least 5 times before going to the golf course. Don't worry about impressing anyone, everyone is there to practice. In fact, you'll be surprised at how many folks need as much practice as you do!

What's available

O Most driving ranges have clubs you can rent -- and some ranges have an instructor on staff or can help arrange lessons.
O The yardage markers on the range tell you how far you're hitting the ball, and make good targets.
O When the weather is a chilly, look for a range with protected, heated tee areas.
O Many ranges have chipping and putting greens so you can practice your short game.

At home on the range

O Be sure to stretch and warm up before practicing.
O Start with a lighter, shorter club (like a 9 iron) and loosen up before you take out the big guns.
O Practice aiming your shots at a target to build accuracy. Developing an accurate drive is often more important than being able to whack the ball and send it a mile.
O The range is a great place to practice shots and make adjustments to your stance and swing.

Before you start swinging

Now that you know a bit about the game, its etiquette, and the course, it's time to think about actually swinging the club. We don't try to teach you how to hit the ball -- you'll need to practice or maybe take a few lessons for that. But, we will give you basic information and some tips so you'll know what to expect.

A **note to lefties:** The illustrations and instructions here are for right-handed golfers. The concepts we explain work for either left- or right-handed players. An interesting fact is that many lefties learn to play golf right-handed. Because the left hand delivers the power in the right-handed swing, lefties playing right-handed enjoy a distinct advantage.

Addressing the ball

This odd term encompasses everything you do when getting ready to swing the club. The address includes your posture, stance, grip, and the position of the club head before the swing starts. It's important to spend the time learning how to address the ball and develop a consistent address -- the foundation of your game.

To: The Cup
1 Stroke Way
Mulligan's Acres

Posture

You want to be comfortable with your back straight and your shoulders slightly bent forward (you don't want to feel stiff like a robot). Your hands will fall naturally just a bit lower than your belt buckle.

The Stance

A square, well-balanced stance will help you hit the ball solidly. As you become more experienced in golf, you'll learn how to change the way you hit the ball by adjusting your stance.

As a beginner trying to just hit the ball, you'll want to stand with your:

☑ feet about shoulder-length apart

☑ right foot straight and the toe of your left foot turned outward at about a 30-degree angle

☑ knees slightly bent and your weight centered on the balls of your feet

Your shoulders, hips, knees, and feet should be in a straight line so your weight is centered and you feel balanced.

You'll place the golf ball in a different position in your stance for the kind of club you are using.

Woods

Position the golf ball toward the front of your stance so the ball lines up just inside your left heel.

Irons

Position the golf ball so it's in a line that is in the center of your stance.

    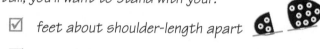

Gripping the club

These pictures give you an idea of the finger, hand, and wrist position while holding the club. The best way to figure out how tightly to hold the club is to think about how you would hold a bird. Firmly enough to keep him under control, but not so tightly that you squash him.

Correct grip

Right V points to your right shoulder. Left V points just to the right of your chin. Ball should go straight.

Grip too strong

Right V and left V point too far to the right. Ball tends to hook to the left.

Grip too weak

Right V and left V point too far to the left. Ball tends to slice to the right.

Taking a swing

There are many good books available whose sole
purpose is to teach you how to swing the club.
So in the next few pages we'll just give you a few
pointers that will help you understand the mechan-
ics and terminology of the swing.

Many instructors will use the clock to help you
break down the components of the swing.   We'll talk
about the swing and how it relates to the clock in 4
parts:

① Backswing
② Downswing
③ Impact
④ Follow-through

The **backswing** is from 6 o'clock up to the top of your
   swing -- somewhere between 1 and 3
   o'clock. Try to keep your knees flexed
   throughout your whole backswing and
   gradually shift your weight from
   center to the right side of your
   body. In fact, about 75% of
   your weight should be on your
   right side by the time the club
   reaches the top of your
   backswing.

The **takeaway** is the part of the
backswing from about 6 to 9 o'clock. As you push
the club back with your left hand, try to keep your
elbows straight but not locked. The area across
your shoulders and down to your hands forms a
rough triangle. Maintain the triangle as you push
the club back. Be careful not to twist the club --
try to keep the club face straight (square).

When you reach the 9 o'clock position, bend your
elbows and bring the club up behind your right ear.
Your upper arm is in a line with your shoulder, and
your right forearm and elbow will
form a 90 degree angle. Your left
shoulder should almost touch
your chin, and your back will
almost face the target.

Flex your wrists until the club shaft is almost parallel with the ground. The club head will be between 1 and 3 o'clock. From this position you're ready to start your downswing.

During the **downswing** you follow the same line that you used to bring the club to the top of the backswing. As you pull the club down, your left hand should be doing most of the work. Keep your knees flexed, and gradually shift your weight to your left side during the downswing.

Increase the speed of your downswing from the 9 o'clock position down. Most of the power in the downswing comes between the 9 o'clock position and 6 o'clock (impact).

Impact is when the club face hits the ball. Be sure to keep the club face square as it hits the ball so it sends the ball in a straight path.

Tip: Remembering to accelerate the club during your down-swing from the 9 o'clock through the 6 o'clock position is important for beginning players.

The **follow through** completes the line of the down-swing after impact. Raise the heel of your right foot as your weight shifts to the left and let your arms and hips follow the club through the shot. The toe of your right foot will be pointed down and your right knee, belt buckle, and right elbow should point to the target. By the time the swing is finished, most of your weight should be shifted to your left side.

Swing checklist ☑

As you're addressing the ball and getting ready to
swing the club, run through this checklist.

Address and stance

☑ Keep a relaxed, comfortable posture.

☑ Your feet should be about a
shoulder width apart.

☑ Balance your weight so it is
centered on the balls of
your feet.

☑ Keep your shoulders,
hips, and knees
square to the target.

☑ If you are using an iron,
the golf ball should be
in the center of your stance.

☑ If you are using a wood, the golf ball should be
slightly forward of the center of your
stance -- just inside the heel of your left
foot.

☑ Grip the club firmly but not too tightly.

☑ In your grip, the right hand V points to your
right shoulder; the left hand V points just
to the right of your chin.

Backswing

- ☑ Transfer your weight to the right side of your body as you push the club back.

- ☑ Keep your knees slightly bent throughout the backswing.

- ☑ The club shaft should be almost parallel with the ground at the top of your backswing.

Downswing and impact

- ☑ Pull the club down smoothly with your left hand doing most of the work.

- ☑ Gradually shift your weight back to your left side.

- ☑ Accelerate your swing from the 9 o'clock position through impact.

Follow through

- ☑ As you follow-through with the club, your right knee, belt buckle, and right elbow point to the target.

Short game

As you get closer to the green, there are times when you need to adjust your swing and hit short shots. The two places this will happen most are when you're chipping and when you're putting. Use the chip shot to get the ball onto the green. Once the ball is on the green, you'll putt it into the hole.

What kind of chip shot do I use?

The kind of chip shot you use depends on what kind of terrain is between you and the green, and how far the ball has to travel across the green to the pin. Also, you don't want to hit the ball so that it bounces hard on the green. A hard landing may cause the ball to bounce and travel too far or in a direction other than what you had planned.

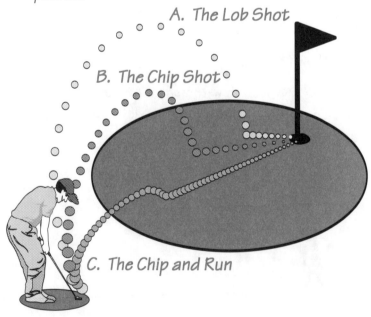

A. The Lob Shot

B. The Chip Shot

C. The Chip and Run

A. The lob shot

The lob shot is considered the most difficult chip shot to control because the ball goes higher into the air -- and is more likely to bounce erratically when it lands. But, you may have to use it to avoid hazards near the green. Use a high-lofted sand wedge for a lob shot.

B. The chip shot

The normal chip shot is a compromise between the lob shot and the chip and run. Use the normal chip when there is some distance or rough terrain between you and the green. This shot is a bit easier to control than the lob because the ball doesn't go as high into the air. Use your 9 iron or a pitching wedge for a chip shot.

C. The chip and run

Beginners will probably find that the chip and run is the easiest chip shot to hit. The ball has little loft and doesn't bounce as much when it lands and rolls across the green -- giving you more control. Use an iron (maybe a 7 iron) for the chip and run shot when you are pretty close to the green.

Putting the ball

Because the etiquette on the green is as important as swinging the putter, we've covered this subject in Section 1, The green.

What about golf lessons?

Here are some questions to consider when signing up for golf lessons:

Where is the lesson given?
Private Golf Club
Public Golf Course
Driving Range
Retail Golf Shops
University or City Recreation Department

How many people are in a class?
If you want individual attention, a private lesson is generally worth the added cost. Sometimes it's fun to schedule lessons back-to-back with a friend.

Group lessons are also fun, and are generally less expensive than private lessons.

How much do the lessons cost?
Call around and compare costs. Depending on the coach's qualifications and temperament, a few extra dollars a week might be worth it.

Finding a good instructor

Choose a golf instructor like you'd choose a friend -- golf is supposed to be fun. Don't be afraid to change coaches until you find someone who is qualified and that you like. And, once you find a good coach, stick with him or her.

Where not to find a good instructor:

Neighborhood or Office Know-It-All.

Significant Other (sometimes also known as the Significant Know-It-All).

As always, try to get recommendations. Remember, being a good player doesn't guarantee that the person is a good teacher. Shop around.

Getting the most from your lessons

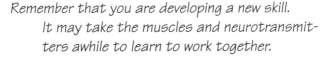

Warm up before the lesson starts. Try to limber up before you start swinging.

Take a few practice shots if you can.

Remember that you are developing a new skill. It may take the muscles and neurotransmitters awhile to learn to work together.

Be sure to ask questions if you don't understand something.

Right after a lesson, recap what you've learned. You might want to write the most important points down for later reference.

Try to practice what you've learned as soon as possible.

There might be over a dozen clubs in your bag. Which one should you use for this shot?

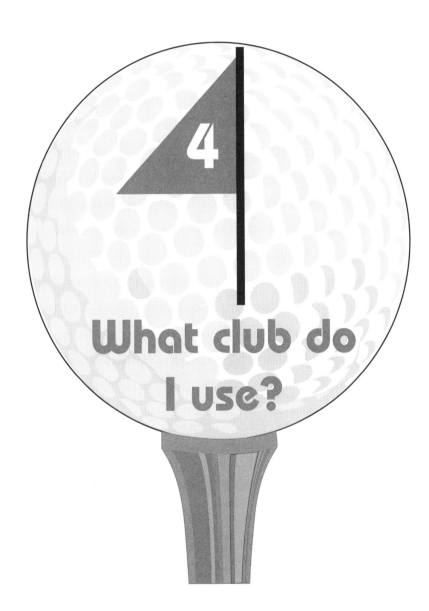

4

What club do I use?

Choosing the right club for the shot

As you play more golf, you'll find that there are clubs that work best for you in certain situations. In this section we give you some ideas to help you get started. You might also want to ask for advice from your golf companions as you play the course.

Teeing off - Generally, a beginner should start off by using a 3 wood. The 3 wood offers good distance and is relatively easy to control. The driver (1 wood) is generally used by more advanced players. It will give you more distance, but it is harder to control. On shorter holes, you might be even better off using a 3 iron.

Approach shots - You can use either an iron or a wood. It's a matter of personal preference.

Trouble shots - Hitting into a hazard can cause trouble. Check out the specialty clubs section to see what clubs might help.

Chipping - When you're within about 40 yards of the green, you might want to break out one of the wedges.

On the green - Here's where you use the putter. Practice, practice, practice.

The chart on the next page helps you figure out what club to use.

Approximate club distance in yards

This table gives you the approximate club distance in yards. You may need to practice to hit these distances consistently.

While you're on the driving range, note how far the ball generally goes when you use certain clubs. That will help you gauge what club to use when you're out on the golf course.

Club	Men	Ladies
Irons		
1	225	185
2	210	170
3	195	155
4	180	140
5	165	125
6	150	110
7	135	95
8	120	80
9	105	65
Pitching wedge	90	50
Sand wedge	75	40
Lob wedge	60	30
Woods		
1 (driver)	235	195
3	195	175
5	175	150
7	155	135
9	135	120

Specialty clubs

Until the late 1930s, there was no limit on the number of clubs you could carry. But the practice of carrying a club for every situation got out of hand, and players would go into tournaments with as many as 25 clubs. With no end in sight, the USGA settled on 14 as a reasonable number of clubs to carry -- the limit you're allowed to carry today.

Generally, a set consists of 11 clubs plus the putter. You can carry specialty clubs to bring the number up to 14.

As the name implies, specialty clubs are designed for particular types of shots. Some players feel that specialty clubs really help their game. Others feel that they just clutter up their golf bag. Practice with specialty clubs and see how they work for you.

Specialty irons	Used for
Sand wedge and Lob wedge	hitting the ball out of a sand trap or bunker and for short chip shots onto the green. The angle on the club face is designed to loft the ball high into the air.
Chipper	short shots onto the green. A different club from the pitching wedge, the chipper is sort of a cross between a 7 iron and a putter. The club has the loft of a 7 iron, but is balanced more like a putter.

Specialty irons

	Used for
Driving Iron, 1 and 2 Irons	a drive that requires accuracy and distance. Driving irons offer almost the drive distance of a wood, with the accuracy you can get with an iron. These clubs are considered more difficult to use off the fairway or without a tee.

Specialty woods

	Club is
9 Wood	often used in place of the lower-numbered irons. Some people find that the added mass in the club head makes it easier to get the ball airborne.
7 Wood	very similar to a 9 wood, but it is a little heavier with less loft, and can offer more distance.
4 Wood	smaller, and more lofted than a 3 wood, the 4 wood gives you almost as much distance. Some people feel that it's easier to hit the ball out of a bad lie with a 4 wood.
2 Wood	used in place of a driver, the 2 wood is also called a high-lofted driver. The shorter shaft can give more accuracy with a distance to that of a driver. The 2 wood is considered by some players to be difficult to use without a tee.

Buying golf equipment
can be confusing.
This section gives you
tips on what to look
for and how to shop.

5

Golf equipment
& buying tips

Selecting equipment

Golf bags

Golf bags actually have 2 jobs. A golf bag not only carries your clubs, but it also protects them from the weather and from damage.

Golf bags are designed specifically for the way you intend to carry them. Will you carry the bag, put it on a pull cart, or use a riding cart?

Carry bags are for golfers who usually do not use a cart. Carry bags are generally pretty light, but look for a bag that has enough pockets to carry your stuff. Some bags even have dual-straps so you can carry it like a backpack. You can also buy carry bags with legs that keep the bag upright when you set it down.

Pull cart bags are usually heavier than carry bags and have pockets that are designed for easy access when the bag is on the pull cart.

Riding cart bags are larger and can be like a portable locker. You can carry a lot of stuff with you -- just don't hurt yourself lifting it onto the cart.

Tip: Check out the manufacturer's warranty. Some warranties are much better than others.

Tip: If you have graphite-shaft clubs, you'll want a padded-top bag. The padding protects the club shafts from rubbing against each other and against the hard dividers in the bag.

Golf gloves

Wearing a golf glove gives some golfers a better grip on the club. A glove also absorbs perspiration and prevents blisters.

If you play golf right-handed, buy a glove for your left hand. If you play golf left-handed, buy a glove for you right hand.

Most golf gloves are made of either leather (Cabretta and others), or a synthetic material. Cabretta is a thinner, softer leather. While cabretta is generally more expensive, it is not as durable as the other leathers. Synthetic materials are made for durability, but can limit the feel of the club's grip in your hand.

Tip: Buy gloves a bit snug, but not tight -- they will stretch over time.

Tip: Cadet-sized gloves are wider across the knuckles and shorter in the fingers than regular-sized gloves.

Clothing

Golf clothes should be comfortable and give you enough room to move around. If you're playing at a private club you might want to inquire about the dress code.

Tip: Try to keep a light, waterproof jacket and/or a sweater in your golf bag so you'll be comfortable if the weather changes.

Golf balls

Believe it or not, there is a lot to consider when choosing a golf ball. Beginners are most worried about just hitting the darned thing. But after you've been playing awhile, you'll be looking for the ball that best fits your game.

Golf balls are made of 2 or 3 pieces.

2-piece golf balls are made of an inner core and a cover. 2 piece balls are usually less expensive, more durable, and travel farther than 3 piece balls.

3-piece golf balls are made in many different ways. One of the more common ways is an inner core that is wrapped with strands of rubber and then a cover. Another way is an inner core, a middle layer, and then the cover. Three-piece balls usually offer more spin and control, but may not travel as far. Better golfers can use spin to control the path of the ball in flight and when it lands.

Hard or soft covers

A hard cover ball is recommended for beginners because it is usually less expensive, travels farther, and is more durable. The cover is often made of Surlyn.

A softer-cover ball is generally more expensive and is used by more experienced golfers who don't lose as many golf balls, and can take advantage of the increased control. The cover is often made of Balata.

Compression

Most golf balls are rated by compression (their hardness). You'll see the numbers 80, 90, or 100 either on the ball or on the box. The higher the number, the higher the compression.

If you have a **fast swing**, consider a golf ball with a compression of 100.

If you have a **medium-speed swing**, try a 90 compression ball. Some pros also use the 90 compression ball because they feel they have more control.

If you have a **slower swing**, consider an 80 compression ball.

Old Sol

The higher the temperature, the higher compression golf ball you might want to use -- heat tends to make the ball softer.

ID numbers

The numbers 1, 2, 3, or 4 are printed on the ball. The ID number helps you tell your golf ball from someone else's.

Buying tips

Tip: Ask the shop pro what kind of golf ball is best for your game and level of play.

Tip: Try different brands of golf balls. Buy golf balls in larger-quantity packs after you've settled on a brand that you like. Cost isn't always a measure of quality, and you may get a better value.

Shoes

Players wear golf shoes to help stabilize their
stance when they swing the club.
It seems that everyone will give you
different opinions about what kind of
shoes to buy. Here are some tips:

Tip: Only buy shoes that fit. You'll walk about 4 miles
during an 18-hole golf game. Imagine the nifty
blisters you can get carrying a 20-pound golf
bag for 4 miles in shoes that don't fit.

Tip: Brand names aren't always a gauge of quality.
Look for quality construction. You don't have to
break the bank -- balance price with quality
regardless of brand name.

Tip: Save your warranty and sales receipts just in
case there are problems.

Tip: Morning golfers and golfers who play in a wetter
climate may
want to invest in
waterproof
shoes.
As you can
imagine, soggy socks are no fun.

Tip: Most golf courses won't let you on with the old
spikey spikes. They insist on soft spikes, or
shoes with molded soles (similar to gym shoe
soles, but with better traction). Manufacturers
usually don't tighten the spikes before they ship
the shoes. You'll have to do that yourself. If you
do lose spikes, they can be replaced for a nominal fee, or you can buy replacements and install
them yourself.

Golf clubs

Golf clubs have evolved along with the times. New materials and designs have led to the development of clubs that are much more durable (although the older clubs sure were handsome). The reason there are so many types of clubs is because everyone wants and needs something different.

There are usually 11 clubs in a full set -- starter sets often contain 7 clubs. This table shows which clubs generally come with a full or a starter set.

Club	Full Set	Starter Set
Irons		
3	X	X
4	X	
5	X	X
6	X	
7	X	X
8	X	
9	X	X
Pitching wedge	X	
Putter		X
Woods		
1 (driver)	X	X
3	X	X
5	X	
Specialty Clubs		
Irons 1 and 2		
Sand Wedge		
Lob Wedge		
Woods		
7 and 9		

Golf for Beginners:

As you saw in the table on the previous page, there are 2 types of golf clubs; *irons* and *woods*.

Irons

Originally, all golf clubs were made of wood. In the early 1700s, club makers started developing clubs with heads made of metal. These clubs were generally specialty clubs that were used to get out of trouble spots.

By the late 1800s, irons had become an important part of a golfer's set. Today, irons are more vital than ever. They are designed by computers and made of the latest materials. Generally speaking, irons are used on the fairway and on approach shots. Specialty irons are still around to help you get out of trouble.

Woods

Like we said, up until the early 1700s, all clubs were made of wood. The shaft and the head were often made of different types of wood and spliced together.

Different types of wood reacted differently when the club hit the ball. This gave the clubs their feel -- and everyone had their favorite combination. But, clubs made of wood were fragile. Players often carried two of the same type of club in case one broke. The metal-shafted wooden-head club design became popular in the early 1930s. The metal-headed wood became popular in the 1970s. And, like irons, today's woods have evolved using the latest technology and materials.

Club anatomy

The golf club has 3 parts -- the grip, the shaft, and the head.

Grip

The grip is where you hold the club. It is important that the grip on the club fits your hand correctly. A grip that is:

too large limits wrist movement, and causes the ball to fall short and to the right of your target.

too small forces you to hold the club too tightly and causes loss of control. Also, the club may slide around in your hand when the club head hits the ball -- especially on off-center hits.

Tip: Arthritic players might want to try a grip called a **jumbo grip**. Jumbo grips are thicker -- and a thicker grip puts less pressure on joints and gives you better control of the club.

Tip: Grips will last for about a year (depending on how often you play). Have the grips changed when they look shiny, or if they feel slippery. You can have grips changed for a pretty nominal fee -- your golf shop pro can help you decide when it's time to change them.

Golf club shaft

Golf club shafts are made of different materials and are "sized" for each player. There are a lot of choices out there, but if you know a little about materials and length, you'll be able to work with a golf shop pro to help you decide the best fit for you.

Club shaft materials

Each shaft material flexes differently depending on the speed of your swing. This is called **shaft flex**. Generally, players with a fast-to-normal golf swing need a stiffer golf club shaft than players who swing more slowly.

Steel Shafts - are in general, less expensive and more durable than other types of materials. Steel shafts come in all kinds of flexes that are commonly broken in two basic groups -- **stiff flex** and **regular flex**. Steel-shaft clubs are a good choice for many beginners. In fact, many tour players still use steel-shafted irons in their game because they're considered to be more accurate.

Graphite Shafts - are lighter-weight and usually more flexible than steel shafts. Graphite shafts might be a good choice for players with a slower or a more controlled swing. The flexibility offers more distance with less effort.

Club shaft length

It's as important to choose the right length golf club as it is to buy the correct size shoe.

Golf clubs are sized according to your height, the length of your arms, how you stand when you address the ball, how fast you swing the club, and the club head position at impact.

Golf clubs come from the manufacturer with a standard shaft length. A good pro shop can fit clubs to you. And, you can find shops that will size and adjust used clubs for a small fee. Be sure to call ahead - this service can take a few days.

Tip: It's best to buy the correct shaft style and size for your game today and trade up later if your needs change.

Tip: A player with a slower swing almost always benefits from a lighter-weight, more flexible golf shaft.

Tip: If you break a golf club shaft, you can have the club repaired for much less than a new club costs.

Tip: Sometimes people sell or trade in their old clubs when they buy new clubs. You might be able to find some pretty good deals on used clubs at the pro shop or garage sales.

Club head

The club head is where the golf club makes contact with the ball. The head can be made of alloys, stainless steel, graphite, or even titanium. Stainless steel is usually more durable than other materials -- a good choice for beginners.

Club head sweet spot

The goal is to hit the golf ball in the center of the club head on each swing. The center of the club head is called the sweet spot. Hitting the ball in the sweet spot delivers the maximum distance and highest accuracy for your shot.

Cavity-back heads

By moving weight from the center of the head to the outside, the club head and its sweet spot can be made larger without adding weight to the club. This is called **perimeter weighting**. The majority of clubs made recently use this technology.

Each manufacturer has their own idea about how perimeter weighting can best increase the size of the sweet spot. Try out several brands of clubs before buying.

Oversized-head clubs

An oversized club head offers the same advantages as a cavity-back head does by enlarging the sweet spot. But, an oversized club can be comparatively bulky and may be heavier. Try oversized head clubs before purchasing to be sure they're right for you.

Tip: An oversized-head club may help players who have trouble hitting the ball in the sweet spot.

Tip: If you've been playing for awhile, and notice that you continually hit the ball either too high or too low, ask the shop pro for recommendations on clubs that can help compensate and improve your game.

Before buying clubs

Try to borrow or rent some clubs and go out on the course a couple of times before you buy. You'll have a better idea of what kind of clubs you need or want, and you'll be able to see if you enjoy the game before you sink much money into equipment.

Going to a golf pro shop can be a bit daunting. It's hard to know what to ask and expect. Before taking a field trip to the pro shop, you may want to consider your skill level, your budget, and how much you plan to play the game.

A field trip to the pro shop

The shop pro's job is to make you feel at ease and to help fit you with the right equipment. They should ask questions like:

How long have you been playing golf and how often do you plan to play? If you play a lot, your skills may improve quickly, and you'll be ready for a more advanced set of clubs sooner.

What is your budget? Think about how much you want to spend before you get to the shop.

What kinds of clubs are you using now? If there is a particular brand of clubs that you like, write down the name and ask the pro about them.

How fast do you swing the club? The speed of your swing determines the kind of club shaft you need.

What do you shoot? The pro doesn't want to know if you go hunting, this phrase is golfese for "What is a typical golf score for you?"

Try before you buy

Try on everything before you buy. The shoes must fit, and the clothes should be comfortable. Most golf shops have a hitting cages and putting areas where you can try out clubs. Ask the shop pro about demo clubs.

Buying irons and woods

Tip: Buying clubs is another place where fit, comfort, quality of materials, and warranty factor into how much you should pay.

Tip: Try not to be seduced into buying a certain brand just because of the advertising or popularity.

Tip: When you buy clubs, it's perfectly OK to buy the irons from one manufacturer, and the woods from a different manufacturer.

Tip: Drivers (1 woods) come in different lofts. If your drives are too high or too low, you might want to select a driver with a loft that helps you compensate. The higher the degree of loft, the higher the trajectory of the ball.

Tip: The driver you select doesn't have to match your other woods.

Tip: Down the road you might also want to consider a driver with a lighter-weight shaft. The lightweight shaft is usually more flexible and may give you more distance (with a slight cost in accuracy).

Tip: There's always an adjustment period when you start using different clubs. Try not to panic if you don't play well with your new clubs right away. You just need to practice with them.

There are rules for almost every situation you can think of in the game of golf.

This section explains a few of the most commonly used rules.

6

Golf rules

Common rules

This section gives only a few of the most common rules just to get you started and familiar with the terminology. We'll tell you the things that can cause a penalty, but you'll need to read the USGA Rules of Golf book for the official word.

You can carry up to 14 USGA approved clubs in your golf bag. And you can carry as much other stuff as you want.

If the ball falls off the tee, there is no penalty unless you intended to hit the ball.

If you hit the ball into:

✓ an area where the course is being repaired (called ground under repair)

✓ a puddle on the course (casual water)

You can pick up your ball and drop it one club length away from the outside edge of the area, but no closer to the hole (nearest point of relief). Continue play without penalty. See the Water Hazards later in this section.

When you are hitting the ball out of a bunker (sandtrap), the club head may not touch the ground while you are addressing the ball (called grounding the club).

Out-of-bounds areas are marked by a fence or white stakes. If the ball goes out-of-bounds (see your scorecard for out-of-bounds areas):

✓ count the first stroke,

✓ add another stroke for a penalty, and

✓ hit a new ball from the first ball's point of origin. Count that stroke too.

This is called *losing stroke and distance.*

Out-of-bounds and the provisional ball. If you hit a shot that looks like it might be out-of-bounds, you can tell your companions that you are going to hit another ball (*provisional ball*).

If the original ball has gone out-of-bounds, you:

✓ count the first stroke,

✓ add another stroke for a penalty, and

✓ count the provisional ball as the third stroke.

Play the provisional ball where it lies.

> If the original ball isn't out-of-bounds, you pick up the provisional ball and play the original ball with no penalty.

A ball is considered lost if you can't find it within 5 minutes of when you start looking for it. If the ball is lost: count the first stroke, add a stroke for a penalty, and hit another ball from the first ball's point of origin. You lose stroke and distance.

Water hazards

Water hazard rules apply if the area is marked by red or yellow stakes, or if the ball is not playable. This brief explanation shows how the rules work for regular and lateral water hazards.

We recommend that you look water hazards up in a rule book for a more complete explanation.

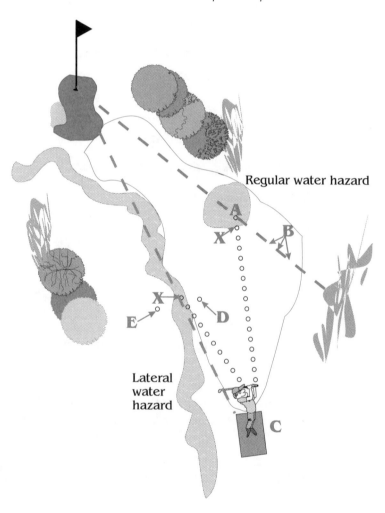

Regular water hazard

Lateral water hazard

Regular water hazards

Regular water hazards should be marked by yellow stakes. If you hit into a regular water hazard, you have these options:

A. If the ball is playable, you can play it where it lies without penalty.

B. You can drop another ball at the point of entry (**X**) or anywhere on a line that goes from that point away from the hole (shown on the regular and lateral water hazards as ▬ ▬ ▬). This option costs a stroke, but not distance.

C. Count the original stroke, add a penalty stroke, and continue play from the point of origin -- costing stroke and distance.

Lateral water hazards

Lateral water hazards should be marked by red stakes. If you hit your ball into a lateral water hazard, you have the same options as you do with a regular water hazard, plus 2 additional options:

D. Drop a ball within 2 club lengths from the point of entry (**X**). The club lengths can be no closer to the hole than the point of entry.

E. Drop a ball in a spot across the hazard from the point of entry but 2 club lengths from the hazard. Again, the club lengths can be no closer to the hole than the point of entry.

If the ball comes to rest on a golf cart path, you can:

A. Play the ball where it lies.

B. Find the spot just off the cart path (**the point of nearest relief**) and drop your ball one club length out but no closer to the hole than **X**.

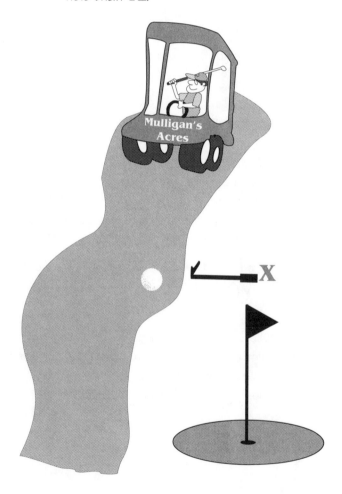

Playing by the rules

Many of the golf rules have to do with shots that lie within a hazard. These strategies are perfectly legal and will help avoid the hazards.

It's important to gauge how you're playing on a particular day. If you're hitting the ball really well, you may feel you can take some risks. If your shots aren't so hot, play it safe and shoot for the middle of the fairways and greens.

When you're hitting the ball into the wind, use a lower-lofted club and a smooth swing.

If the cup is on a severe uphill slope, try to chip the ball a bit short of the cup. It's easier to putt uphill than downhill.

If your opponent puts their tee shot into the woods, do whatever you can to keep the ball on the fairway. This gives you an advantage for the next shot.

If you put the ball into the woods, play it safe and just hit out to the fairway. If you feel lucky, or have a lousy going score anyway, take a chance and shoot out of the woods toward the green.

Watch out for sucker pins. Sucker pins/holes are positioned on the green close to hazards. Plan your shots on the safe side to avoid the hazards. Aim toward the middle of the green.

The Words of wisdom
are tips that you'll find
really helpful.

The Golf lingo helps you
understand and speak
the language of golf.

Words of wisdom & Golf lingo

Words of wisdom

FOR SAFETY SAKE:

IF A STORM COMES UP, OR IF YOU SEE LIGHTNING -- GET OFF THE COURSE AS QUICKLY AS POSSIBLE. Your clubs and metal-spiked shoes make great lightning rods.

REMEMBER, WATER CONDUCTS ELECTRICITY. If lightning strikes a wet surface, the charge can be carried for great distances.

DON'T STAND UNDER TREES WHEN THERE IS LIGHTNING. If a tree is struck by lightning, the charge is conducted to the ground by the root system. If you are standing on top of the roots, you could be conducted into the ground too - INSIDE A BOX.

GOLF COURSES USE CHEMICALS THAT CAN BE POISONOUS. Your golf ball and tees pick up chemicals that are used on the course. Please don't put your fingers in your mouth after handling the ball or tee.

More words of wisdom

Keep all your golf equipment receipts and warranty records for no-hassle returns.

Professional golfers very seldom have matched sets of clubs. Most pros use clubs that they like the best regardless of the manufacturer (unless, of course, the manufacturer is their sponsor). The same applies to you. The disadvantage is that it might be harder to sell a non-matching set of clubs when you decide to upgrade.

Don't be a marketeer. Buy equipment because of its fit and quality -- not because it's well marketed.

Consider using head covers for your woods. Covers will keep them looking new for years.

Some manufacturers supply pro shops with demo clubs for customers to try out on the course or the driving range before they buy. Take advantage of this offer before making purchases.

Whether you buy new or used golf clubs, always have them fitted to you. Playing with clubs that aren't fitted to you is like driving a car with one cylinder out. It may look good, but you don't get anywhere very fast.

More words of wisdom

Your first set of clubs doesn't have to be expensive -- just fitted to you. Buying used clubs is a great way see if you like the game without investing much money. The key is to take the clubs to a reliable pro shop and have them fitted to you. The expense is small when compared with the improvement in your game.

Be sure to buy golf shoes that fit! You'll be walking for miles. Good-fitting shoes are not necessarily the most expensive ones, so try on many different manufacturer's shoes. If you play in the morning or in wet conditions, you should consider waterproof shoes. It takes 2 or 3 days for a pair of golf shoes to dry out. If you play frequently, or in wet conditions, you might want to have another pair of golf shoes so you can rotate them.

Buy golf gloves a bit snug because they'll stretch a little.

All golf pros and instructors will tell you that the best way to lower your score is to practice chipping and putting as much as possible.

More words of wisdom

To save your back, be sure to follow through when you swing.

When you find a good instructor, stick with them. It's a bit like finding a good personal physician. The instructor gets to know you and your habits. Also, everyone has their own ideas about golf. Taking lessons or advice from several folks can be confusing.

When you find a pro shop with competitive prices and knowledgeable salespeople stick with them, especially when buying clubs. If you find a lower advertised price somewhere else, give your favorite shop a chance to match it.

The first time you play on a golf course, ask someone who has played before to go with you. They can help show you the ropes.

It's not finders keepers. If you find a club on the golf course, be sure to turn it in. People spend a lot of time and money picking out and buying the right clubs, and you may have found someone's favorite or lucky club.

More words of wisdom

When lining up a putt, pay attention to the direction
the grass is growing (grain). When the ball is travelling against the grain of the grass, the ball goes
slower. The ball will travel faster if it is moving in the
same direction as the grass grows. You may have to
compensate by hitting the ball a bit harder or softer.

When you go to the driving range, use the grassy areas
to shoot from rather than the mats. It's more like
being out on the course.

If you take your clubs with you on a plane, always put
them in a travel cover or case. The airlines treat golf
bags like luggage.

Golf bag goodies

You might want to carry these items in your golf bag:

Ball markers
Bandaids
Bug repellant
Divot tools
Extra golf balls and tees
Lip balm and sun block
Pencil
Rain suit or umbrella
Rule book
Spare change (there
may be pop
machines out on
the course.)
Spare golf gloves
Towel

Golf Lingo

These are some of the words you might hear on the golf course. We've included them because they have very little basis in the English language.

Bogey train - keep getting bogies and can't seem to make par on a hole.

Bumping the ball - illegal way to play. Moving the ball to give yourself a better lie. Don't do it unless everyone in your party agrees.

Chili dip - cousin of the chunk, and uncle of hitting fat. But usually occurs when chipping. You take such a big divot when chipping that the ball doesn't go very far.

Chunking - chunking is when you take too big a divot before hitting the ball. Taking extra grass slows the club head speed and takes momentum from your shot.

Crusher shot - drive that sends the ball into orbit (or at least that's how it gets described in the clubhouse).

Fried egg - when you hit a shot into the bunker and the ball embeds into the sand -- looks like a fried egg.

Getting up and down - when you use 1 stroke to chip up onto the green and 1 stroke to sink the putt.

More golf lingo

Hitting fat - same as chunking.

Hitting thin - not taking any grass sends the ball like a line drive with little height. Hitting thin may cause you to hit past your target.

Hitting the green in regulation - you reach the green in two strokes below par. If you're playing a par 4 hole, hitting the green in regulation means you take 2 strokes to get onto the green. You can take 2 strokes to putt and still meet par.

Hockey stick - when you take 7 strokes to complete a hole. The number 7 looks like a hockey stick.

Hook - ball curves from right to left.

Lateral shot - same as shank.

Lip out - when the ball goes around the lip or rim of the cup and doesn't go in. Bummer.

Mulligan - the name of our company. It's also an illegal way to replay a lousy shot. Mulligans aren't quite kosher, but if everyone agrees, it can make the game a bit more fun.

Pick, clean, and place - on days where the course is wet or muddy, the course will sometimes declare that it's a pick, clean, and place day. You are allowed to pick up the ball, clean it, place it back, and continue play.

More golf lingo

Playing it down - playing the ball where it lies.

Point of relief - the nearest point away from trouble.

Provisional ball - a second ball that you hit in case your first ball went out-of-bounds.

Shank - a word that is never uttered aloud. It means hitting the ball off the hozel of the club -- sending the ball horizontally.

Slice - ball curves from left to right.

Skulling the ball - same as hitting thin.

Snowman - when you take 8 strokes to complete a hole. The number 8 looks like a snowman.

Summer rules - same as playing it down.

Texas wedge - when you use your putter to get the ball onto the green instead of using your chipper.

Three putt - it takes 3 strokes to get the ball into the hole. Bad news.

Whiff - you swing and miss the ball. Yikes!

Winter rules - winter rules are followed when the course is in bad condition. You can move the ball a bit to give yourself a better lie.

Worm burner - when you hit a shot that skims across the grass so fast that the worms duck.

Index

1 and 2 irons, 55
2 Wood, 55
2-piece, 60
3-piece, 60
4 Wood, 55
7 Wood, 55
9 o'clock position, 41
9 Wood, 55

A

ace, 27
approach shots, 52

B

backswing, 41
Balata golf balls, 60
ball is considered lost, 75
ball mark, 21
birdie, 27
bogey, 27
budget, 70
bunker, 12

C

cabretta golf gloves, 59
cadet gloves, 59
carry bags, 58
casual water, 74
chip and run, 46
chip shot, 46
chipper, 54
chipping, 52
club sets, 70
correct grip, 39
course par, 30
course rating, 29

D

divots, 9
double bogey, 27
double eagle, 27
downswing, 42
dress codes, 7
driving iron, 55
dying into the hole, 20

E

eagle, 27
Etiquette, 7
even par, 27

F

fairway, 12
flag, 12
flag, moving, 22
follow through, 43
fore, 9

G

golf bag off green, 21
golf links, 4
green, 12
grip too strong, 39
grip too weak, 39
ground under repair, 74
grounding the club, 74

H

hole handicap, 28
honor, 21
hook to the left, 39

I

impact, 42
individual handicap, 28
instructors, 48
Introduction, 1
irons, 53, 63, 64
irons, shot distance, 16

J

jumbo grips, 65

L

lefties, 37
Let the games begin, 3
line of site, 23
lob shot, 46
lost ball, 75

M

mark your ball, 22
match play, on scorecard, 13
mind your manners, 8
move quickly off the green, 23
move the flag, 22

N

net score, 29
note to lefties, 37

O

Object of the game, 5
on the green, 52

P

par, 12, 27
perimeter weighting, 68
pick, clean, and place, 14
pin, 12
pin sheet, 19
play through, 10
playing through the green, 4
playing winter rules, 14
point of relief, 74
provisional ball, 75
pull cart bags, 58
pulling the pin, 22
putt out, 21

Q

quadruple bogey, 27

R

rake the bunkers, 10
reading greens, 19
renting a cart, 8
riding cart bags, 58
rough, 12
Rules, 5

S

sand traps, 10
sand wedge, 54
sandtrap, 74
scorecard, 11
shaft flex, 66
slice to the right, 39
soft spikes, 62
specialty clubs, 63
speed of play, 8
spikes, 62
Surlyn golf balls, 60
sweet spot, 68

T

takeaway, 41
team score, 32
tee box, 12
tee marker color, 15
tee time, 6
teeing off, 52
the beach, 12
The game of golf, 4
Tips to know before going to the course, 6
triple bogey, 27
trouble shots, 52

U

unofficial handicap, 29
USGA Rules of Golf, 74

W

water hazards, 12, 76
what do you shoot, 70
Where is the lesson given, 48
where is the lesson given, 48
where to stand, 23
woods, 53, 63, 64
woods, shot distance, 16

Y

yardage markers, 16

Mulligan's Press
Golf for Beginners: The Official Survival Guide, a book that every beginning golfer must read! We've gotten a lot of really nice feedback.

Golf Magazine, April, 1996 issue
...fun, easy to read, short; and designed to help neophytes over the inevitable self-consciousness and intimidation...making it good for advanced beginners.

Robert Mitchell, Owner, Nevada Bob's Golf Shop
I recommend this book to all my beginning and intermediate skill level customers.

More comments:

Green Meadows Golf Club, Larry Murdock,
Head Professional
It's jumping off the shelves...everybody really loves the
way it explains the game and the great tips.

Mac and Terry McDermott, Owners,
Pro Golf Golf Shop
Finally, someone put down in print what we tell our
customers every day. Golf for Beginners: The Official
Survival Guide is an entertaining book that covers
the game in a way beginners can understand ...

We hope you enjoy the book!